❁ The Satirical Rogue

❧ The Satirical Rogue
on Poetry

ROBERT FRANCIS

THE UNIVERSITY OF MASSACHUSETTS PRESS 1968

❦ Foreword

I take this opportunity to thank the editors and secretary of *The Massachusetts Review* for their kindness in assigning copyright to me in seventeen of these essays that first appeared in *The Massachusetts Review*.

I wish to thank also the editor of *The Virginia Quarterly Review*, Miss Charlotte Kohler, for her kindness in assigning copyright to me in seven of these essays first appearing in *The Virginia Quarterly Review*.

To the Jones Library of Amherst, Massachusetts, and its entire staff, as well as to the Robert Frost Library of Amherst College and its staff I am grateful for innumerable courtesies and services. Both institutions opened to me their treasures and made me feel at home during my years of research on this volume.

Finally, to my wife, Patience, I lovingly acknowledge an eternal debt. Without her ceaseless encouragement and inspiration I could not have pursued this work to its conclusion. Busy all the while with household tasks and the rearing of seven children, she was nonetheless always ready to come instantly to my side. Unassisted she typed and retyped the entire manuscript fifteen times. The merits of this book are hers; only the faults are mine.

ROBERT FRANCIS
Fort Juniper
Amherst, Massachusetts

✿ Contents

POLONIUS: I'll speak to him again. What do you read, my lord?

HAMLET: Words, words, words.

POLONIUS: What is the matter, my lord?

HAMLET: Between who?

POLONIUS: I mean, the matter that you read, my lord.

HAMLET: Slanders, sir: for the satirical rogue says here that old men have gray beards, etc.

Hamlet, II.ii

✿ The Satirical Rogue

❦ Be Brutal

A friend comes with poems to be criticized. "Be
brutal," he says. "Be ruthless. Tear them apart."

You smile and take the poems in your hand. Be
brutal? Somehow you never feel brutal towards a
poem, even when it obviously deserves brutality.
Toward a human being, perhaps, now and then, but
not toward a poem. It lies there on the page so
helpless to defend itself, so at your mercy. After all,
it is only a few inoffensive words put together in a
certain way.

No, you could never be really brutal with a poem.
And you suspect that he knows you couldn't. What
he really wants and hopes is that you will love his
poems and praise them. But he wants to keep as far
as possible from seeming to. He wants your praise to
surprise him. He wants to say he didn't think the
poems were very good himself. Ideally he himself
would like to be brutal while you triumphantly
defended his poems. "Be brutal," he says.

Pulling yourself together, you resolve to be helpful,
tactful, and honest, all at the same time. You recall
the critics of *your* poetry who were only honest.
Particularly one man who lit his pipe and took a puff
and said, "The trouble with this poem—" And took
another puff and said, "The trouble with this poem—"
And took another puff and said, "The trouble with
this poem—"

3

So you ask your friend if he would be willing to leave the poems with you for a day or two. You want to brood over them.

"Okay," he says. "But be brutal."

❧ Either Or

"After talking with Uncle Charles the other night about the worthies of this country, Webster and the rest, as usual, considering who were geniuses and who not, I showed him up to bed," says Thoreau in his *Journal* for January 1, 1853, "and when I had got into bed myself, I heard his chamber door opened after eleven o'clock, and he called out, in an earnest, stentorian voice, loud enough to wake the whole house, 'Henry! was John Quincy Adams a genius?' 'No I think not,' was my reply. 'Well, I didn't think he was,' answered he."

Whether Henry and Uncle Charles agreed on any other worthies, there was something they seem to have agreed on implicitly and that was that a man is either a genius or not a genius.

Isn't this a little odd in a man who measured accurately the varying depth of Walden Pond and the varying thickness of Walden ice? Did it never enter his immensely capable head that genius, though it cannot be measured like ice and water, is nevertheless something that varies in amount, like water and ice, from spot to spot and individual to individual? That while most people have none to speak of and a few have it in abundance, some people have genius in small amounts? Did it never occur to him that John Quincy Adams was a great man with possibly a small amount of genius? Less than Daniel Webster but more than John Doe down the road?

Another night Henry and Uncle Charles may have discussed the poets, who were major and who minor, putting all the poets into their respective hemispheres separated by a line as inexorable and as imaginary as the equator.

❈ On Looking Like a Poet

Some poets look like poets, other poets do not, but those who do do not all look the same. There was the big blue beret and the small red beard. There was also the great white head and the black overcoat slung over the shoulders like a cloak. Sometimes a poet looks like a poet without trying.

Interesting to speculate why some poets do and some poets do not, why some want to and others don't care or even want not to. If looking like a poet can be an advantage, it can also be a disadvantage. The difference depends on what sort of poet the poet is looking like, and also on where he happens to be. For some poets it would take courage to look like a poet, but the courage might prove unrewarding.

Self-expression is important to all poets, and looking like a poet is one form of it. If a poet happens not to be writing fine poems or even any poems at all, looking like a poet may be almost the only form of self-expression he has.

❧ Blood

"You have a stain on your white shirt," said my friend. "Looks like blood which the laundry couldn't take out."

"It's blood all right," I said. "I got it at a recent poetry reading."

"My God!" he cried, "are poets now wielding knives and rapiers?"

"Not the poets but their poems," I answered. "This fellow's were so violent and bloody there was danger of getting spattered if you sat too near the front."

"I suppose you didn't object to the blood and violence," he went on, "but only to the getting spattered."

"Maybe," I murmured.

❧ Defense of Poetry

I knew a poet once who defended poetry. He defended poetry as he would have defended womanhood on the highway at night. Actually he did more than defend poetry, he defended individual poems. Thus he went beyond Shelley and Sidney who were content to defend poetry in general and in the abstract. One might almost say there never was a poem this poet wouldn't defend. None was too poor or frail for him to champion. Frailty rather than beauty it must have often been that roused his chivalry.

If a slip of a highschool girl wrote an "Ode to Spring," this poet instantly became protective. Any poem, any poem at all, by the fact of its being a poem was precious and therefore precarious.

He was a rare bird. Possibly no one today feels and acts just as he did.

Certainly not I. I would say that a poem worth defending needs no defense and a poem needing defense is not worth defending. I would say it is not our business to defend poetry but the business of poetry to defend us.

✿ Lyric as Arrow

It goes without saying that an arrow to wound must be well aimed; to wound cleanly must be sharply pointed; and to fly accurately through the air must be light, slender, and tough. May not much the same be said of a lyric?

Of any brief poem that we today call a lyric? And doesn't the scarcity of these arrow-like qualities help to explain why I am so often bruised by a poem, so seldom wounded cleanly?

And I want to be wounded. Like Sebastian I bare my breast to the arrows. I would gather them in. I am already sufficiently bruised.

✿ Black Eye

A drawing of Pablo Neruda by Seymour Leichman (reproduced in the *New York Times Book Review* of July 10, 1966) shows the Chilean poet with a pronounced black eye. But it was only recently that the significance of this feature came home to me.

What is a poet, after all, but someone to whom life has given a black eye? How better could you define him?

One poet will simply report the fact, as vividly as he can. A second poet will go beyond reporting to express an acceptance or a reconciliation in the sense that Margaret Fuller accepted the universe. A third poet is the rebel boasting that if life has given him a black eye he has done the same to life.

Poets, of course, also write poems. But without the black eye no writer of poems is ever quite the poet.

❧ In Her Own Right

Whenever I hear of someone who is a poet in her own right or in his own right, I am curious to know in what other way a person can ever be a poet.

Take Cornelia Crumb, for instance, wife of the poet Crumb, who we are informed is a poet in her own right.

The implication is that Mrs. Crumb is a poet in her own right in addition to being a poet in a right not her own. But if being the wife of a poet confers quasi-poethood on Mrs. Crumb, why isn't this in her own right too, since Crumb is without question her husband?

If I were writing about Mrs. Crumb I would say: "Mrs. Crumb is a poet too." Or, "Mrs. Crumb, like her husband, is a poet." Or, "Mrs. Crumb is a poet herself."

But no one else thinks as I do. Let anybody else write about Mrs. Crumb and we are assured that she is a poet in her own right.

❊ On the Exquisite Air

All artists love to talk about themselves and their art, but poets in their public readings seem unable or unwilling even for a few minutes to separate their art from themselves.

They give us details of inspiration, composition, and publication. They go behind the scenes and take us with them. What we have is nothing less than a complete poet's-eye view of his poems.

Sometimes the commentary and confession come in such an engulfing stream that the poems are quite submerged and only dart in and out of sight like swimming fish.

Why poets do so much talking in public I really don't know. In his studio a painter may or may not chat about his paintings; but when those paintings are hung in an exhibit, does he post himself at the door to give every visitor a personally conducted tour?

My own notion of a poetry reading is quite different. I want the poet to talk about his poems as little as possible, and not so much about the poems as about something one step removed. The voice in which he does his talking unfortunately is the same voice the poor poems must borrow. The more we hear him the less we may be able to hear them.

I should like poems hung, one at a time, like Japanese pictures, on the exquisite air, each poem surrounded by space and silence.

❧ Distinction

Finding themselves at last together in one book, the poems accepted each other almost instantly. After all, were they not a true family, having one and the same father?

Those that had had the honor of previous publication in magazines and those that were appearing in print for the first time soon forgot their differences of status.

All except one little poem—and you couldn't tell merely by looking at it why it was this little poem and not any other little poem in the book. But it was a fact that this little poem had first appeared in the *New Yorker* and it could never quite forget it.

❧ Teacher

When I look back at the poetry teaching I have done or tried to do, I see it in the form of a round pie cut in six sections.

The first slice is what I told them that they already knew. This generally pleased them since it made them feel like advanced students.

The second slice is what I told them that they could have found out just as well or better from books. What, for instance, is a sestina?

The third slice is what I told them that they refused to accept. I could see it on their faces, and later I saw the evidence in their writing.

The fourth slice is what I told them that they were willing to accept and may have thought they accepted but couldn't accept since they couldn't fully understand. This also I saw in their faces and in their work. Here, no doubt, I was mostly to blame.

The fifth slice is what I told them that they discounted as whimsey or something simply to fill up time. After all, I was being paid to talk.

The sixth slice is what I didn't tell them, for I didn't try to tell them all I knew. Deliberately I kept back something—a few professional secrets, a magic formula or two.

So my pie is all used up and what teaching have I done?

Yet we always had a good time in class. Drawn together by a common interest and pursuit, we enjoyed one another's company. Especially we enjoyed laughing together.

❧ The Muse

When people speak of The Bard everyone knows
they mean Shakespeare. But when people speak of
The Muse which Muse do they mean? For there are no
fewer than nine Muses, as who hasn't heard? Nine
daughters of Zeus and Mnemosyne, the goddess of
Memory.

Calliope, *epic poetry*
Clio, *history*
Erato, *erotic poetry*
Euterpe, *lyric poetry*
Melpomene, *tragedy*
Polyhymnia, *religious poetry*
Terpsichore, *the dance*
Thalia, *comedy or bucolic poetry*
Urania, *astronomy*

After eliminating Clio, Terpsichore, and Urania,
we still have six. Why do people persist in talking as
if there were only one Muse when there are six of
these divine women ready, each in her proper field
and jurisdiction, to come to the aid of the deserving
poet?

❧ Poetic License

How many years has it been since I heard that phrase? And just what does it mean, or did it mean? Does it, did it, refer to a general latitude permitted poets in their use of language, or did it refer to something more specific? I think I used to know. But that was long ago.

What did my high school English teacher have to say about poetic license? Was it poetic license when a poet said "marge" for "margin"? Or was it something else? I'm sure she knew and made us know; but though I remember some things she taught us as if it were yesterday, I have forgotten what she said about poetic license.

I remember very well the Harvard Comma, for instance. When three or more words are used in a series, the first two are separated from each other by a comma. The last two are separated (as well as connected) by the word "and." Should there be a comma here too? For years the question had hung fire, some authorities saying one thing, other authorities another. But now Harvard had spoken. There *should* be a comma before the "and." Red, white, and blue. This was the Harvard Comma.

Hila Helen Small was an extraordinarily devoted and conscientious teacher. It would be no exaggeration to say no human being could have been more so. I remember her as entirely gray—not only hair and eyes but manner and speech. She moved swiftly through the corridors with a soft swish and a faint jingling of keys.

Actually she was not quite so severe as she looked. Her severity was not so much toward human beings as toward what they said and wrote. Once, for instance, she appeared suddenly in a room that had been left temporarily teacherless. There she stood in perfect silence, her gray eyes fixed on a small misbehaving girl. "The boy in back of me hit me with his ruler," said the child in defense.

What would Avenging Justice say to this? What punishment would be meted out?

"Never say 'in back of,' say 'behind,' " said Miss Small.

Early in life she had taken a vow that no ungrammatical or otherwise incorrect expression should ever pass her lips and none ever had. We, her pupils, could watch the unending struggle, the pursed lips, the poised teeth. Miss Small never said anything bright, or profound, or amusing, but, by God, she never said anything incorrect.

Today when the attitude toward language is almost altogether permissive, we smile at such perfectionism. But we may be missing something, just the same.

There was excitement in Miss Small's correctness. It was like a game. Would she or wouldn't she ever make a slip?

But what did she tell us about poetic license? I'm sure it was the most unlicentious kind of license imaginable. I still use the Harvard Comma regularly, though during my five years at Harvard I never once heard it mentioned.

✻ Scenes

I

A: Did I see a poem of yours somewhere recently?
I: It's possible.
A: Where could it have been?
I: What magazine was it in?
A: I don't remember.
I: About how long ago was it?
A: I've forgotten.
I: Do you recall the title?
A: No.
I: Or what the poem was about?
A: No.
I: Or anything about the poem?
A: Oh, it doesn't make that much difference.
    I just wanted you to know I'd seen it.

II

B: Did I see a poem of yours somewhere recently?
I: Impossible.
B: I'm sure it had your name.
I: Must have been the other Robert Francis who
    writes poetry.

✥ Poet as Bird

"This," says The Yale Series of Recorded Poets of
Yvor Winters, "is a field recording made in the poet's
own locale."

✤ Art of Slow Reading

The more we race over the surface of the earth and the faster and farther we fly above it the more important now and then to do a little walking.

In an age of speed reading, poetry has the virtue, in addition to whatever other virtues, of slowing us down. A shrewd doctor might prescribe the reading of poetry for a variety of contemporary ills.

Poetry, of course, has always been something to read slowly, just as a fine wine has always been something to sip. But today, as everyone knows, there is another reason for slow going. In the past you grasped a poem fairly quickly and lingered over it for enjoyment. Today you often have to linger over a poem to grasp it at all.

By slow reading we generally mean not only a slow pace but a frequent pausing and a going back to read again. Rapid reading is measured by so many words a minute or a second. It would be absurd to try to measure slow reading. Yet one might say sensibly that in a flight to Chicago he spent the two hours reading one short poem.

I hope it was not a mere puzzle-poem. A puzzle-poem might keep one reading all the way to the moon and back. Ideally one would spend most of the two hours not so much trying to penetrate the poem's shell as its depth. One would muse over not only what the poem was saying but what the poem was doing.

Slow reading of this sort is a double test: a test of the reader's resources and a test of the poem's. Poem asks the reader: "Do you get all I am giving?"
Reader asks the poem: "How long can you keep me interested, keep me reading? All the way to Chicago?"

✿ Word-Count

DAPHNIS: Seen any of the so-called word-count poems that Robert Francis writes?

DAMON: Not that I know of. What's the idea?

DAPHNIS: All the lines in a poem have the same number of words. It might be seven to a line, or five, or perhaps only three.

DAMON: I couldn't get excited about that.

DAPHNIS: It doesn't have to be exciting to be useful. Question is, can it help produce a fine poem?

DAMON: Daphnis my boy, fine poems are sometimes, by the grace of God, produced in spite of rather than because of artificial frameworks.

DAPHNIS: That's a debatable point, Damon. I mean, what you call *in spite of* may actually be *because of*. A poem gets written in spite of something or other. Because of in spite of, you might say.

DAMON: God, what quibbling! But it's not quibbling to say that counting words is too mechanical.

DAPHNIS: Any more mechanical than counting feet? Five feet to the line? Five words to a line?

DAMON: But feet are meter and meter means rhythm and rhythm is the lifeblood of poetry. Counting words is like counting sausages.

DAPHNIS: All right, I grant you that counting words
does nothing for the rhythm. But how
about counting syllables? As Marianne
Moore does? Don't some pretty brilliant
poems get written that way? Because of or
in spite of?

DAMON: Oh, if you have to count something,
syllables will do. They're short.

DAPHNIS: But why not words? Playing the long ones
against the short ones?

DAMON: That's precisely what all poets do anyhow.

DAPHNIS: Damon, old boy, we're arguing. But the
proof of a poem is in the reading.

DAMON: Have you got one on you?

DAPHNIS: Yes. I copied it at the library this morning.
(Takes out a folded paper and hands it to
Damon.) It's typical Francis.

ICICLES

Only a fierce
Coupling begets them
Fire and freezing

Only from violent
Yet gentle parents
Their baroque beauty

Under the sun
Their life passes
But wait awhile

Under the moon
They are finished
Works of art

Poems in print
Yet pity them
Only by wasting

Away they grow
And their death
Is pure violence.

DAMON: Sort of brittle, I'd say. But then you'd have
to remark that so are icicles.

DAPHNIS: Damon, old scout, you're hard to please.

DAMON: And you, Daphnis, I sometimes think are
too easy.

✤ Half-God

How Socrates must have surprised that drinking party over two thousand years ago when he told them that the god of love was not a god who had everything, but rather a half-god always longing to complete himself.

Isn't a poet typically the same? If his wife can't think of anything to give him for Christmas, it isn't because he already has everything, but only because what he doesn't have his wife can't give him.

Or perhaps he has no wife. If he is so poor that he goes hungry, he will probably somehow or other be rich in love. Or if he is starved for love, he will doubtless sit down to a good dinner every day.

If he had everything, what impulse would he have to write? If he had nothing, what would he write about?

❀ Garret

It has just occurred to me, after all these years, that
my basic lack as a poet may have come from my not
having a garret to live in and write in, to sleep in and
dream in.

Where better than in a garret can a poet be both
high and humble? An integral part of life and yet
above it all? From a garret he can look out on treetops
and across to other garrets. He can look down on the
bustling world and yet not too far down. In spring and
summer and fall he can listen to the rain's commentary
close to his head, and in winter he can watch the
lengthening icicles as they dazzle in sun or glint in
moon.

If some philanthropic foundation, or indeed if my
country itself, wishes to grant me some signal boon,
rather than gold or travelers checks let them give me
a garret to live in and write in, to sleep in and dream
in.

But what am I saying? This is not the way to get a
garret. To get a garret—if haply there are any garrets
left in the modern world—one should find it himself
and pay the rent with money he himself earns. That
would be good in every way you look at it.

✿ Love Me, Love My Poems

Long, long ago this was my good fortune. When my first book was published, everyone who knew me knew that book. Everyone who was betting on me bet on me as a poet. Everyone who loved me loved my handiwork. Not that I made demands on my friends. Their pleasure in my flowering was as spontaneous as if the flowering were their own.

How different it is now. How very, very different now.

❦ It Really Isn't

It isn't expensive to be a poet. A pencil and piece of paper are all the equipment needed to get started. Homer managed with less.

A pencil or pen and a few pieces of paper. Then an envelope or two and some postage stamps.

Pencil or pen or typewriter. A portable typewriter isn't expensive if you can make one last a lifetime.

You may fancy writing in an Italian villa or a French château, but the poems you write there will be no more immortal than those written in your bedroom at home.

Nor do you need very much of that most precious of all items, time. Odds and ends will do. Evenings, early mornings, noon hours. Sundays, holidays, and when you sprain your ankle.

It's quite otherwise with a painter. Paints, brushes, and canvasses cost money, and a painter can't very well paint in his bedroom. Still less could a sculptor sculpt in a bedroom. An architect may need a whole suite of rooms in an office building. And as for the composer, what can he do without a grand piano and somewhere to play it?

No, if a poet can support himself he can support his poetry. If he can keep himself fed, his poems won't starve.

So, when you come right down to brass tacks, a poet

doesn't really need the aid, assistance, subsidy, and support that munificent philanthropy stands ready to grant him. In this, isn't he lucky?

If you insist on giving him something, say, a free year in Rome, it may turn out that what you have chiefly done is to add to his baggage.

✿ Bad Poem

There are two approved ways of turning thumbs down on a poem. (1) You can say it isn't a poem at all. It's merely verse. It's doggerel. It's mere rhetoric. Or (2) you can call it a bad poem.

Either way disposes of a poem effectively, but only in the second way can you properly send it to hell. A poem that isn't a poem at all, a poem that is merely verse or doggerel or rhetoric, does not necessarily deserve eternal torment. After all, verse has its place. Even doggerel has its place. Rhetoric may not have any place today but it used to have and so enjoys an honorable background. But a bad poem obviously deserves to be cast into outer darkness where there is weeping and gnashing of teeth.

When you call a poem bad, you pick it up firmly by the ear between thumb and forefinger and toss it into the pit. As you do so you give a shrug, a wry smile, a grimace, as if the poem were not only bad but smelt bad.

If somebody comes along and tries to tell you that there are many, many poems too good to be called bad and too bad to be called good, and that within bad and good there are infinite degrees of badness and goodness, and that a poem may be rather good in some respects and rather bad in others, and that goodness and badness depend on criteria about which poets and critics will never agree, and that a poem might better be called poor, or feeble, or faulty, or unfulfilled than bad—if anybody tries to talk that way, you can be sure he is quibbling, hedging, evading, unwilling honestly to face the responsibilities of judgment.

It is all quite clear and definite. Bad poems are bad, and poems not bad are good. And just as there are bad poems and good poems, so there are bad poets and good poets. A bad poet probably never writes a good poem, but some admittedly good poets have confessed to writing some bad poems. For a good poet to confess writing a bad poem tends to prove three things: (1) his candor, (2) his critical acumen, and (3) the goodness of all his good poems.

But why split hairs? Have not the estimable authors of *Understanding Poetry* put the whole matter in a nutshell? "Bad poems," they say on page 391, "are made by bad poets like Kilmer and good poems are made by good poets like Yeats, Shakespeare, Milton, etc."

❧ With and Without Honorarium

A poet is like a physician in at least one respect.
Sometimes he is paid for his services and sometimes
not. He may be well paid one night and not at all the
next. A physician of course is glad to do work free, or
at least he takes his charity cases in stride. The same
thing may well be true of a poet.

When he is working for pay, receiving perhaps
several hundred dollars for a reading or lecture,
people can't do enough for him. He is met at the
airport and taken to someone's home for entertain-
ment overnight. He is guest of honor at a dinner
before his reading and at a party afterwards. If he has
been permitted to incur any expense at all, he will
probably be reimbursed for it in addition to his
honorarium. Finally, after a leisurely breakfast the
next morning, he is taken back to the airport. Again
and again he is thanked for coming.

What happens when he is working free? It is
probably a local occasion and he is allowed to get
there by his own devices. At the door he is met by
someone who tells him where he can leave his hat
and coat. The audience proves just a trifle cool. The
poems that last night seemed to give pleasure give less
pleasure now. After it is all over, someone thanks him.
He goes out and gets into his car and starts home. On
his way he begins to wonder whether he should not
have thanked the audience for their kindness in coming.

❧ Lounge

God forbid I ever have to give a poetry reading in a
lounge, a lounge where the listener sinks out of sight
and sound in some deep-bosomed overstuffed divan.

If anybody ever drops a pin during my reading,
for God's sake let me be where I can hear it!

❧ Frost as Mugwump

Years ago I heard Robert Frost define a mugwump as a little bird balancing on a twig with his mug pointing one way and his wump the other. Wasn't Frost himself a perfect illustration?

He laughed at educators, and was one. He twitted scientists but kept up with what they were doing. He was pro-art and anti-art: an artist to his fingertips when writing poems, but a plain man and no nonsense on the platform speaking those poems. Also a plain man and no nonsense speaking *in* those poems. As for religion, you can make out as good a case for Frost the skeptic as for Frost the believer.

He was in favor of walls and he was scornful of walls. In "Mending Wall" the speaker kids his neighbor for insisting on repairing an unnecessary wall; but the speaker keeps right on doing his share of repairing nevertheless. That was not the only fence that Frost was on both sides of.

Did his mugwumpism help him as a poet? I wouldn't venture to say. Some great poets have been middle-of-the-road, others have been extremists. But one thing certain is that his mugwumpism helped Frost as a wise man. In the popular mind a wise man can't be an extremist. If he is so broadly and centrally located that he speaks, or seems to speak, for everybody, then he is a wise man indeed.

Of course Frost's definition of mugwump is far from accurate, and Frost probably only picked it up somewhere. Strictly speaking, a mugwump is a member of one political party who now and then switches his vote to the other party. This is what many Republicans did in 1884 to help elect Grover Cleveland. A mugwump by rights is a little bird that flits back and forth between two twigs. Or that changes his direction on the same twig.

Frost had good reason to be interested in mugwumps, for in politics he was close to being one in the true meaning of the word. A passionate Democrat at nine years of age, he helped elect Cleveland. At eighty-six he not only helped elect another Democrat for President, he helped inaugurate him. But in between, during those New Deal years, that was another story.

My guess is that Frost would not object to being called a mugwump. The word was pure American even before the coming of the white man. In the Algonquin tongue it means "big chief." No, Frost would not object. I can almost hear him chuckle.

✿ Poetry as a Source of Suffering

Only in the secrecy of my own heart do I dare confess how much suffering poetry has brought me over the years. To confess to anyone else would open me to the charge of ingratitude both to the Muse and to my fellow poets. I am really a little ashamed to confess even to myself that what supposedly should have been a source of pleasure has so often been otherwise.

My suffering is of three sorts. My own poetry has made me suffer, and for this, of course, I myself am exclusively to blame. Then I have suffered from what other people have said or not said about my poetry. Finally, there is the suffering from other people's poetry. For this, surely, I am not wholly responsible.

When I speak of the suffering that my own poetry has brought me, I am not thinking of the struggle of creation, for this is a happy kind of agony if it results in something worth agonizing over. I am thinking rather of those poems that brought a glow of achievement one night but disintegrated under my eyes the next morning. Or of those poems that ought to have disintegrated but somehow found their way into print.

What I suffer from in other people's poetry is many things, according to poet and poem. But perhaps most of all from the too obtrusive presence of the poet himself. I want him near enough to see and hear vividly, but not necessarily so near as to feel his breath in my face.

One could argue that it is a chief virtue of poetry today to cause the reader to suffer. To make him accept his suffering and even to enjoy it. Only by prodding him, shocking him, and making him wince can a poet waken and revitalize his reader. I suffer; therefore I am.

If this is so, then I can only say that I wish I could have enjoyed my suffering more.

❧ By the Rude Bridge that Arched the Flood

That such a little jewel of a poem as Emerson's "Concord Hymn" should be an occasional poem is something of a paradox. Though occasional poems occasionally pass muster, they are very very seldom jewels.

Part of Emerson's secret, I venture, was his casualness with this as with his other poems. "Toy with the bow," he said elsewhere, "but hit the white." He did not tear his hair over a poem as Lowell did over his "Commemoration Ode." When "Concord Hymn" was sung to the tune of "Old Hundred" by a band of youths and maidens at the completion of the Battle Monument in Concord on July 4, 1837, Emerson was not even present. He was away visiting in Plymouth.

Nowhere in his fourteen-volume journal or in any of his six volumes of letters, so far as I can find out, did he mention the poem. It was mentioned by his mother in a letter to her son William.

Had Emerson been asked by his fellow-townsmen to write something for the occasion? Or had he himself taken the initiative and offered his services? Whichever the case, the poem, like most occasional poems, was doubly occasional, written both for and about the occasion.

Now the chief trouble with writing for and about an occasion is that you become so impressed with the importance of the occasion that you are likely to become impressed with the importance of your writing about it. Something big, obviously, is called for.

One thing, aside from his good taste, that helped save Emerson from bigness was the fact that the poem would be sung to a simple hymn tune. Though "Old Hundred," in the singing, must have weighed down Emerson's winged words, in the writing the old tune probably served at least to keep the poem lean.

✿ Production Belt

A poem comes onto the moving belt sometimes as a piece of paper with a few words scribbled on it, but many a poem begins its journey less tangibly as a mere hint, a hunch, a possibility, and may travel for considerable time and distance before pen, pencil, or typewriter comes into operation.

During overt composition a poem may travel a surprisingly short or long time and distance. Yet when "finished," its travel along the belt may have hardly more than begun. The marketing phase begins. And this too may take the poem a short or long time and distance.

If it is accepted for magazine publication, it goes on moving patiently along the belt, unable to do much of anything except to be patient, until the magazine comes out. A small flurry of activity may accompany this event; the arrival of a check, its cashing, and the paying of one or two small bills.

Still the poem rides on. In due course it becomes one in a book of poems and, if accepted by a publisher, enters a phase of bustling and varied activity on the belt. After publication activity continues though spottily—the arrival of reviews, requests to reprint, and invitations to the author to give poetry readings. Also from time to time there may arrive a small check.

Of course a poem may be thrown off the belt or fall off at any point. We are assuming that this poem stays on for as long a ride as possible. Further transformations await it, such as its reappearance in a volume called *Selected Poems*, and later in a volume called *Collected Poems*. Even this is not the end.

Having followed one poem in its long journey, we might look at the whole belt with many poems riding on it in various stages of progress. During a typical day the poet will be at work now at one location along the belt and now at another. Poem *A* he may be sending to a magazine, Poem *B* may be still in the polishing and testing stage, Poem *C* he has not finished writing, and Poem *D* is a gleam in his eye.

He is at his best when he has poems well spaced along the belt, and it does him good to move from one working position to another. To have poems past and poems future, poems coming and poems going, is to feel confident, secure and full of life. A hitch anywhere along the line can interfere with progress everywhere else. If and when the belt slows down and stops moving, poets have been known to do desperate things. But as long as the belt moves and there are poems to the right of him and poems to the left of him, the poet has no trouble keeping busy. He has a full-time job.

❦ Labels

They wrote to ask what label I wanted under my
picture. I looked at my three predecessors of the
previous year. One was "Poet, teacher, and editor."
The second was "Poet, teacher, and literary critic."
The third was "Poet, poetry anthologist, and editor."

Why were poets, I asked myself, never satisfied to
be poets? Why were they always something else and
something else? As if a poet had to have three persons
to be on firm ground?

What label did I want? "Poet." Nothing more.

Of course, there were all sorts of other labels I could
have added. "Property-owner, tax-payer, car-driver,
typist, letter-writer, book-reader, traveler, gardener."
But I suspected that the more other things I was the less
poet I might be. Besides, long after I had stopped traveling and paying taxes I might still, God willing, be a poet.

So I said, "Poet." Period.

A bit bold, perhaps, for one who when he began to
be a poet didn't want to be called one. Before my first
volume I avoided the label whenever I could. If people
called me poet seriously, I didn't deserve it. If not
seriously, I preferred not to be a stock joke. But that
was long ago.

"Poet," I said.

When the publication appeared, I looked to find
myself. There was my picture all right, but under it
this label: "Lecturer, critic, teacher, poet."

❀ Somebody–Nobody

Somebody, hearing that Emily had called herself a Nobody, decided to be a Nobody too—not just any Nobody but a Nobody who really was a Somebody, like Emily.

✿ Santayana, Columbus, and Samuel Eliot Morison

Though poets have long been hailed as Truth-Speakers, their reputation as liars has been no less persistent. Isn't it precisely when a poet draws breath to utter a Truth that he is most in danger of lying?

Take Santayana. In his celebrated sonnet he says of Columbus, "To trust the soul's invincible surmise/Was all his science and his only art."

This statement is not only untrue, it is less than flattering to Columbus. Had not Columbus been a shrewd, experienced seaman using every scrap of scientific knowledge available and every trick of the navigator's art, he never would have reached America. If you have any doubts of this, I refer you to another Harvard professor who wrote about Columbus, Samuel Eliot Morison.

That Columbus had a soul I do not question, or that his soul had a surmise or that the surmise was invincible. I insist only that soul was not the whole story.

Today a poet has perhaps a better chance of speaking the truth than poets had in Santayana's day, Truth-Speaking in poetry having largely gone out of fashion.

❧ The Pathetic Fallacy

It sounds like something nobody would wish to be guilty of. Who wants to be fallacious? Who wants to be pathetic?

This unhappy phrase was coined by Ruskin. Though he does his best to make clear that the pathetic fallacy is all right in its place and may even be very beautiful and moving, his best is not good enough. A readiness to form categories and make judgments does not altogether conceal the confusion in his thought. The more he particularizes and qualifies the more we too become confused. Indeed he gives us more fallacies than the one he gives a name to.

According to Ruskin, when a poet misrepresents the outer world or distorts what we are pleased to call reality, he may be moved either (1) by "wilful fancy," or (2) "by an excited state of the feelings making him, for the time, more or less irrational." It is the second fallacy that Ruskin calls "pathetic."

But having drawn this distinction, he proceeds to muddy the waters. Here is his illustration of fallacy number one, and here also is one of his illustrations of fallacy number two, the pathetic. The reader might amuse himself by trying to tell which is which.

> The spendthrift crocus, bursting through the
>   mould
> Naked and shivering, with his cup of gold.
>   [O. W. Holmes]

> The one red leaf, the last of its clan,
> That dances as often as dance it can.
>
> [Coleridge]

Another illustration he gives of the pathetic fallacy is this:

> They rowed her in across the rolling foam—
> The cruel, crawling foam.   [Kingsley]

This is a clearer case, granted, but even here we want to ask questions. Is the voice that speaks in these lines irrational or morbid? Are the men who row the drowned girl home irrational or morbid? The evidence is that they are not. Grief-stricken they may be and grim, but perfectly lucid. They know the sea. They know the sea can drown. They have encountered this thing before. How can they have any illusion? If the sea is cruel as a cat or snake, it is cruel not because it is imagined to be a cat or snake but because it is the sea.

The voice speaking in these lines is not only lucid but calm. The rowers go on with their grim task. There is no fallacy here at all.

What Ruskin calls falsification or distortion is best interpreted neither as wilful fancy nor as unhinged reason, but as the poet's central desire to find a language powerful enough to match his vision.

49

Ruskin's chief interest in the pathetic fallacy seems to be his claim that only poets of the second order indulge in it freely. Poets of the first order—Homer and Dante—are strong enough to get along without it, indeed are all the stronger for getting along without it.

Later on we are told that the pathetic fallacy is characteristic of modern poets and painters. The ancient and medieval mind was unfriendly to it. So, after building up his case for poets of the first order, he pulls it down. Homer avoided the pathetic fallacy not because he was a poet of the first order but because he lived in an age when everybody else felt and did the same. Likewise with Dante.

Ruskin cites with enthusiasm one modern poem that avoids the fallacy. Is it by a poet of the first order? Casimir de la Vigne in his poem "La Toilette de Constance."

Poor pathetic fallacy.

❧ The Man Who Wrote One Poem

It was an enviable position he was in. He could be a poet or not a poet according to mood and company. He could say yes or no and prove it.

If somebody said to him, "But you write poetry, don't you?" he could say, "Actually I've written just one poem in my life, and one swallow doesn't make a summer."

At another time in another mood he could, if he wished, murmur casually, "That reminds me of a little poem I once wrote." He wouldn't have to say it was his only one.

Of course he knew his poem by heart. It was instantly available.

Should anybody be so ungracious as to look down his nose at the little poem, the author could always defend himself with, "But what do you expect of a *first* poem?"

Presumably he could have gone on writing other poems like other poets. But he knew when to stop. Having proved that he could do it, he had the sense not to go on repeating himself.

Enviable chap.

✤ Dame Edith

If poetry really needs something extra and special, some flash of color, some dramatic heightening, then, better than all the prizes and gold medals and fancy dinners and White House flourishes, would it be to persuade Dame Edith Sitwell to return from the realm of shades. To see her once again regally or ecclesiastically robed and seated in a great chair made to simulate a throne, looking like Elizabeth the First or Lady Macbeth or Robert Graves' portrait of the White Goddess.

And should she find her audience annoying, to hear again her voice lifted in denunciation. To hear again perchance what she is reported once to have told an Edinburgh audience:

"No one has ever been more alive than I am. I am an electric eel in a pond full of flatfish."

❊ Duty

Strange things poets sometimes say, and not in our own day only. Wordsworth, for instance, beginning his "Ode to Duty," addresses her as "Stern daughter of the voice of God."

Now a daughter of God is something we can grasp, but what are we to make of a daughter of the voice of God?

One would suppose that the voice of God itself would serve very well as Duty. Wordsworth, however, obviously wanted something feminine to apostrophize, something like the Muse if not the Muse herself. Yet if he had called Duty the daughter of God, he would have got himself into theological hot water. For God to have a Son is of the very essence of things; but for God to have a Daughter would smack of paganism.

The Greeks were realistic. Every goddess or demi-goddess had both father and mother. The Muses were daughters of Zeus and Mnemosyne (Memory). Our Cherubim and Seraphim, on the other hand, and all the orders of the angelic host are asexual or epicene. Though the angels have masculine names, in Christmas pageantry their roles are unhesitatingly taken by high-school girls in white cheesecloth and flowing hair. Wordsworth's solution was theologically safe, and as poetry it has passed muster these many years.

Long ago when Wordsworth was my favorite poet

and I knew the "Ode to Duty" by heart, I never once questioned the parentage he gave her. If in those days a skeptic had raised his eyebrows, I would doubtless have defended Wordsworth by saying that poetry was not meant to make sense but to lift up the heart.

Today few odes are written, and very very few to Duty. Indeed, the very word Duty is heard on our lips how seldom, how seldom.

❦ Poetry as an Un-American Activity

If the notion ever got around that poetry was an un-American activity (as in some respects it certainly is) and that poets were dangerous people (as some of them surely have been and are), and if instead of being encouraged with prizes, awards, gold medals, fellowships, and other subsidies, they were penalized and even suppressed—

So that to escape fines and prison sentences and loss of good name and employment as college teachers, most poets stopped writing poetry altogether—

Except when, on very rare occasions, a poem so insisted on being written that the poet yielded to temptation despite all risks and wrote a poem he was willing to die for—

If, in other words, poetry almost disappeared from the earth and only occasionally in some out-of-the-way place bubbled up like a pure mountain spring—

❀ Too Busy for Both

If it is true that not everyone who goes to a poetry reading is invited to the party afterwards, it is equally true that not everyone at the party has been to the reading. People too busy for both poetry and drinks tend to prefer the latter. At one stroke they escape both the poetry and the obligation to say something pleasant about it.

They remind me of those insects—bumblebees, I believe—who instead of working their way down into a flower for its nectar, sometimes cut a hole at the base of the blossom and so get their nectar the easy way. Though botanists disapprove the practice, I cannot find it in my heart to condemn it.

❧ The Messy Muse

"You see," my friend said the other day, "you're not really a poet at all."

He paused for my reaction. Finding me receptive, he proceeded.

"To begin with, you're too orderly. Poetry is not so much order as disorder. A sweet disorder, to use Herrick's phrase, though I grant that today the disorder is more often bitter or sour than sweet. Poetry is actually a blend of order and disorder. You—you're just order and nothing else. The muse of poetry is the Unconscious and she is notably messy."

Was there the slightest possible smile on his lips? Or was their curve noncommittal? Even I who knew that expression so well could not be sure.

"In the second place, you're too sane. Lovers, madmen, and poets—wasn't it Plato who pointed out their kinship? Even if a poet can't manage to be mad, he should at least have his ups and downs. If you ever had any ups and downs, I never noticed them."

His candor held me spellbound.

"In the third place, you're not a rebel. You're not against things—the universe or society or the administration. You never learned to rage. I'll be damned if you ever even wanted to learn. You're too philosophic. You were born to be a philosopher, and got sidetracked somewhere along the line into poetry."

"I see," I said.

"Of course," he concluded, "I don't deny, I'd be the last person in the world to want to deny, that you've turned out some rather remarkable poems."

❧ Mr. Eliot's Cats

When T. S. Eliot assembled the volume called *The Complete Poems and Plays of T. S. Eliot*, he placed between *Murder in the Cathedral* and *The Four Quartets*, *Old Possum's Book of Practical Cats*.

How comes it that I never heard or read any comment on this extraordinary juxtaposition?

Between his greatest play and his last great lyric achievement, precisely here we have "Old Deuteronomy" and the others.

Was this Eliot's humor? Or was it his humility? Or both?

He might, of course, have omitted "Old Possum" from *The Complete Poems and Plays* altogether. Or, including it, he might have put it at the end, perhaps in smaller type. Instead he put it where he did. Evidently the assembling of his collected poems was not an ordeal for Mr. Eliot.

When we take a writer very Seriously, Seriously with a capital S, we run the risk of taking him more Seriously than he takes himself. One recalls Max Beerbohm's little Mary Augusta (later, much later, Mrs. Humphry Ward) in red ruffled dress, with hands folded demurely behind her, looking up at her uncle, Matthew Arnold, towering above her with an enormous grin on his face, and saying:

"Why, Uncle Matthew, Oh why, will not you be always wholly serious?"

✿ Non-Criticism

Scornful of non-persons, e e cummings was happy writing his non-poems and giving his non-lectures.

Presumably he felt that a person ought to be a person and failed when he was something else, whereas a poem ought to be something else and failed when it was a poem.

❧ Wild but Polished

For these exhilarating words we are indebted to the jazz pianist, Dorothy Donegan, and to *Time* magazine which on November 3, 1958 published a brief interview with her.

Even without the accompanying photo (caught obviously in a wild moment) it would be easy to picture her. A little toss of the head, "I'm wild." Then another toss, "But I'm polished." She was speaking, of course, of her piano playing. But what wouldn't a poet, any poet, give to be able to say the same of his poetry?

Miss Donegan didn't say she combined freedom and form. She is not a lady professor. She took the extreme of freedom, wildness, and the extreme of form, polish, and let the two strike sparks.

The American word "wild" is full of wonderful ambiguities. A wild boxer or baseball pitcher is no good, but the ski coach who called a certain youth "a wild man on skis" meant only praise. "Wild" is lack of control, and "wild" is such virtuoso control that the wild man can take beautiful chances. No one will misunderstand Miss Donegan.

Even within the good kind of wildness there are differences. There is the leaping, soaring wildness of a wild animal or bird; there is also the perfectly quiet wildness of wild fruit whose most notable distinguishing feature is flavor. Some wild poems are deer or hawks. Others are wild strawberries in the grass, wild apples in the woods.

This is not to say the wilder the better. Can a poem be too wild? This depends partly on your taste: you may prefer only a trace of wildness, wildness as a trace element. It also depends on what you mean by wildness. If a poem is so wildly leaping that it leaps permanently beyond your grasp, that is one thing. But flavor is another thing and it is hard to see how a poem can have too much.

Can a poem be too polished? This also depends on your taste and also on what you are polishing. Contrary to what is often said, polishing doesn't always result in polishing away. Are you polishing a piece of chalk or a diamond?

If you are only wild or only polished, you face the danger of too much. But if, like Dorothy Donegan, you are both wild and polished, you are fairly safe and very good.

The poetry we call modern has been no more polished than the poetry that preceded it (and sometimes distinctly less so), but no one can deny that it has been wilder with every sort of wildness.

❁ Goddess

Robert Graves in his celebrated book pictures the
White Goddess as a blood-sucking vampire luring men
to destruction. Mr. Graves' unqualified devotion to the
Goddess cannot be other than touching. His devotion,
indeed, is like that of the male spider fated to be
consumed by the female immediately after the act of
love. Since the female is often overeager to begin
before the male has finished, he offers her a small
insect wrapped in a veil to appease her appetite for
the moment and divert her attention.

Some scholars have questioned the existence of the
White Goddess. I fear she is all too real.

✿ Advantages in Being a Poet

It is the disadvantages, of course, that we hear most about today—the dwindling audience, the swelling publication costs, and so forth. Yet there are still advantages in being a poet.

Take security, for instance. Who has more? If he has put the best of himself into his poems, then the best of himself is to a large degree safe. He is safe not only because what he most wants to keep safe is in his poems, but also because the poems themselves are compact enough to be kept safely. Unpublished they can be filed in a fireproof cabinet or vault. Published in book form they have the greater safety of wide distribution in libraries. Compare this situation with a painter's eternal problem of where to keep his unsold paintings safely, accessibly, and not too expensively.

The days drift by. The poet writes a small poem. And then another poem. They add up. They become a small volume. Then another volume. The volumes add up. *Selected Poems*, perhaps, and possibly *Collected Poems*. The poet is now an old man with one book containing his life.

Or suppose he never has a volume published. In some safe place, as safe as possible, he keeps a loose-leaf notebook containing, neatly typed, all his poems that have stood the test of nonpublication.

A second enviable advantage a poet has is his

freedom to work on a poem almost anywhere he happens to be—train, bus, plane, waitingroom, park bench, bed. Since an impulse may strike unexpectedly and does so more often than not, he is lucky to need only the common pencil in his pocket and a piece of paper. Even if he is dependent on a typewriter, a pencil will do to sketch a poem or revise one already down on paper. Nobody around him need know what he is doing. He might be a traveling salesman figuring his accounts.

Odd times and places are not only possible for poetry, they may actually spur it. Jet travel can be very favorable, thanks to the freedom from interruption, the steadiness of the plane, the sense of being on top of things, and the powerful hum that blots out lesser noises. A painter or composer in flight might sketch a figure or a theme; the poet can do the whole poem.

Another advantage, though one that some poets might not admit, is the willingness of people to make allowances for him just because he is a poet. He is not required to know anything in particular. He is not supposed to be efficient like other men. Social position with him, if he has any, does not depend on possessions. If he looks a little shabby, why not? He is a poet. He may drive an old car with dignity. He may even walk. In short, he may be comfortable, if he is willing. And being comfortable and noncompetitive (except in his poetry, of course) he has little or nothing to come between himself and the writing of his next poem.

✤ No Poem so Fine

No poem is so fine that some critic can't damn it
if he has a mind to. Poetry, unlike light verse which
plays safe and does all the laughing without getting
laughed at, is defenceless, takes all the risks, goes out
on a limb, sometimes very far out. The more a poem
is a poem the closer it plays to the absurd, trusting
the reader to tell the difference.

No poem is fine enough to be safe. A critic can
always maul it or pooh-pooh it if he has a mind to.
Poems have not learned jujitsu or karate. They go
naked and trusting.

On the other hand, no poem is too wretched for
some critic (if he has a mind to) to hail as a gem.

❧ Woman with the Tape Recorder

She arrives with a pleasant bustle, the woman with the tape recorder. She has taped so-and-so and so-and-so and so-and-so, all of them my betters. Now she has come to tape me. Is she doing me a favor? Not exactly. At least she doesn't seem to imply that she is. Am I doing her a favor? Not exactly either. Her manner does not suggest that I am. It is simply that poets these days are being taped, taped as unprotestingly and unceremoniously as maples in sap season are tapped.

Unlike poems in print which are protected by copyright and contract, poems on tape enjoy a large freedom. They may be played by the possessor to a live audience, or played over the air to a larger audience, or played intimately in the boudoir, or played not at all. The tape recorder captures not only the poet's poems but the poet's voice as well. When the woman with the tape recorder leaves, it may seem that she has just about captured the poet himself.

This time, however, things turned out a bit differently. Taper and poet got to talking pleasantly about one thing and another until it was time for her to go. The poet remained untaped, untapped.

✿ Emily and I

The year that Emily Dickinson was born (1830), my father's father, Daniel, was a lusty young man of twenty who in that very year left Ireland for America by sailing ship. When Emily was fifteen, Daniel entered the Harvard Medical School from which he graduated two years later. When Daniel died in 1867, after twenty strenuous years as a country doctor in Nova Scotia, Emily was at the peak of her poetic power or a little beyond, and my father was one year old. When Emily died in 1886, my father was a lusty young man of twenty, and I was born fifteen years later.

✤ Silent Poetry

The idea of silent poetry or silence in poetry used to puzzle as well as fascinate me. I wanted such poetry to exist but I couldn't quite see how if by "silent" was meant "wordless" or "non-speaking."

Recently it has occurred to me that a silent poem may be like a silent man. By a silent man we ordinarily mean not one who doesn't speak at all but one who speaks little. Little enough to impress us with his non-speaking. Why couldn't a silent poem similarly mean one that impresses us with what it leaves unsaid? A poem not only less talkative than most prose but less talkative than much poetry?

Silent people are usually silent by nature. Silent poems have to achieve their silence. It is possible that a silent person may say little simply because he has little to say. The silence of a silent poem is pregnant.

A poem benefits doubly by its component of silence. The silence itself is delightful and at the same time provides the perfect foil for what is spoken. A silent poem comes to us on a white background.

How is silence achieved? A very short poem, like a cry on a still night, makes the surrounding stillness more vivid by breaking it. A longer poem may have somewhat the same quality if it seems to be made up of very short poems, that is, has a fragmentary character. Or if transitions and connections are omitted.

All clean prose has a degree of silence; but poetry may begin where prose leaves off, omitting not only all unnecessary words but even some words that might be thought necessary.

A poem that presents an object or scene or situation without comment approaches the silence of painting or sculpture. Any formality is silent since it contrasts with mere noise and chatter. Yet the very casual can be silent too, if its manner is one of musing rather than of talking. Ultimately silence in poetry depends on restraint and control. The more a poem has of either or both the more silent it is.

If you say that all poets love words, you might add that some poets love words so completely they trust them to the limit, while other poets love words no less but distrust them a little. The latter are the silent poets.

The word-trusting poet may be charmingly exuberant. He may be Irish. I am far from ready to say that only silent poems are fine poems.

Like a silent person a silent poem stands aside. Stands aside from chatter and chance conversation. Stands aside from all shouting. Stands aside also from artiness and calculated effect which we call rhetoric. Stands aside even from song, for song is even less silent than speech, the singing voice sounding continuously whereas the speaking voice is broken by innumerable minute silences.

Since the general tone of poetry in our century has shifted from singing to speaking, we may all of us have been moving one degree nearer silent poetry.

❧ Hard

When Robert Frost said he liked poems hard he could
scarcely have meant he liked them difficult. If he had
meant difficult he would have said he didn't like them
easy. What he said was that he didn't like them soft.

Poems can be soft in several ways. They can be soft
in form (invertebrate). They can be soft in thought
and feeling (sentimental). They can be soft with excess
verbiage. Frost used to advise one to squeeze the water
out of a poem. He liked poems dry. What is dry tends
to be hard, and what is hard is always dry, except
perhaps on the outside.

Yet though hardness here does not mean difficulty,
some difficulty naturally goes with hardness. A hard
poem may not be hard to read but it is hard to write.
Not too hard, preferably. Not so hard to write that
there is no flow in the writer. But hard enough for
the growing poem to meet with some healthy
resistance. Frost often found this healthy resistance in
a tight rhyme scheme and strict meter. There are
other ways of getting good resistance, of course.

And in the reader too, a hard poem will bring
some difficulty. Preferably not too much. Not enough
difficulty to completely baffle him. Ideally a hard
poem should not be too hard to make sense of, but
hard to exhaust its meaning and its beauty.

"What I care about is the hardness of the poems.
I don't like them soft, I want them to be little pebbles,

but placed where they won't dislodge easily. And I'd like them to be little pebbles of precious stone—precious, or semiprecious." (Interview with John Ciardi, *SR*, March 21, 1959.)

Here is hard prose talking about hard poetry. Frost was never shrewder or more illuminating. Here, as well as in anything else he ever said, is his flavor.

What contemporary of his can you imagine saying this or anything like it?

In 1843 Emerson jotted in his journal: "Hard clouds and hard expressions, and hard manners, I love."

❀ Poetry as Stuff

Recently an Ohio woman, a stranger to me, wrote to ask a favor, and graciously ended her letter with the remark: "I love your stuff."

I had almost forgotten the word, and how, long ago, one young poet would say to another: "I'll show you my stuff." Much as a boy might say to another: "I'll show you my marbles if you'll show me yourn."

As a synonym for poetry "stuff" doubtless has its virtues. It is down-to-earth, tough, and utterly unpretentious. When you call your own poetry stuff, you aren't making any claims for it. It may be awful. Or it may be rather good. You aren't saying. Let others say.

On the other hand, when you call somebody else's poetry stuff, you aren't implying or insinuating anything. It may be damn fine stuff indeed.

Yet somehow I never could bring myself to use the expression. Stuff? Stuff was precisely what my own poems were not. To other people, perhaps, but not to me. If sometimes other people's poetry seemed to me no better than stuff, that, of course, was all the more reason for not using the word.

No, no. And yet—to be perfectly honest with myself—while I've been talking about it, I wonder if I haven't been growing a little fond of the word after all?

❧ Lowell

"Weak-winged is song," sang Lowell at the commencement of his "Commemoration Ode." At this point he may have given thanks to have made so promising a start, for the ode, as he himself tells us, was proving one big headache.

But though the words ring out, do they speak the truth? Song may be ever so weak in everything else, weak-headed and weak-handed, weak-kneed and weak-footed, but surely not weak-winged. Wings are what song is strong in. Yes. Wings make song song, make song sing.

Poor Lowell! And after all his labor!

❀ Poet on the Platform

A song composer doesn't sing his songs in public unless he is also a singer. A poet reads his poems in public as a matter of course.

To sing well enough to sing in public is acknowledged to be an art requiring both aptitude and training. Is it an art to read one's poems in public?

The answer varies. Yes. No. Yes and no. It varies according to who is answering the question. It also varies according to the poet who is reading.

Those who say, "No, the reading of poetry aloud is not an art," may add, "unfortunately." Or they may add, "Thank God." Poetry reading, according to a prevailing sentiment, is not only not an art, it had better not try to be. Let it keep as far as possible from art, artifice, artiness, artificiality, and every other nonsense. The poet is asked to be natural, nothing less and nothing more. If he stutters, well then let him stutter. If he lisps, let him be true to his lisping. Let him stand before us as God made him.

The poems he has written may or may not be art. He himself may regard them as art or as non-art. They may be extremely artistic or extremely inartistic. But when he reads them to us or speaks them for us, let the words come from his lips as effortlessly and artlessly as leaves coming out on a tree.

With fundamental and unmistakable honesty he

stands before us, asking us nothing, promising us nothing. "Just as I am without one plea."

We who have come to hear him may or may not be able to hear. If we hear, may or may not understand. If we understand, may or may not enjoy.

He stands before us as God made him, stark naked, yet curiously unembarrassed. Nor are we who have come to hear him particularly embarrassed either.

Anyone not wholly content with this situation, anyone dreaming of a poet's voice presenting poems with the clearness with which picture glass presents pictures, can comfort himself with the thought that though the situation may not be ideal it might easily be worse. If the poet whom God made took it into his head to remake himself a little, to improve his reading, the result would not necessarily and invariably be improvement. Perhaps it is awareness of this misfortune that makes an audience prefer to risk a poet reading without art rather than with. The faults for which God is responsible are easier to forgive than those for which the poet himself is exclusively to blame.

✿ Redress of Grievance

Something a friend told me long ago keeps bothering me a little. Among the reviews of his first book of poems was one especially unfriendly. It wasn't so much that the reviewer condemned the book as that he seemed determined to condemn it. What he said was imperceptive as well as hostile. Could he have even read the book?

A few years later reviewer and author found themselves together at the MacDowell Colony. The reviewer was in a friendly mood. He asked the poet to forgive him for his review, explaining that he had written it to vent a grudge scarcely related to the book at all.

An interesting point. Is private apology due restitution for public wrong?

If a reviewer has simply changed his mind about a book, he may want to say so in print when he has a chance, and this in fairness both to the book and to himself. Whether he condemned a book too harshly or praised it too lavishly, he might welcome any suitable occasion for setting the record straight. But he would hardly be under any obligation to do this. All of us are changing our minds about everything all the time. Having set a record straight, we might have to keep on indefinitely.

What bothers me is not a mistaken judgment but

a miscarriage of justice. What does the Bill of Rights say about this? What are a poem's civil liberties under the Constitution?

❀ To Dislike Poetry Is Not Necessarily to Disparage It

Isn't it naive to assume that what makes a fine poem necessarily makes enjoyable reading? Intensity, honesty, articulateness? Who doesn't have among his acquaintances an intense, honest, and articulate person whose visits one would be happy to be spared? Emerson once observed that people should be taken in small doses. Much poetry today gives us the poet himself or herself in massive doses.

One might read poetry as one takes a good medicine, a good bad-tasting medicine, as a stimulant, perhaps, or as a purgative. But having taken a few doses, one may not wish or need to take more.

To dislike poetry is not always a confession of inability to understand it. Some poems, some fine poems, like some fine people, one might dislike all the more the better one got to know them.

❦ Chaos

"There is simply not enough chaos in his soul," says the *Irish Times* reviewer of a certain Irish poet.

Closing my eyes I can imagine he is talking about me, chaos being something I too am weak in.

What can a poet do, what can he hope to achieve, in whose soul chaos is deficient?

❀ First Person Singular

After all the innovations and inundations and revolutions in poetry in our century, the breaking down and sweeping away of what had long been thought the foundations, the boundless liberty that poets including the most esteemed, indeed the most esteemed most of all, have helped themselves to and reveled in, the all-inclusive and now unchallenged liberty to write anything one pleases in any way he pleases—it seems hardly possible that anyone however isolated and superannuated could ask such a question.

"Do you consider it permissible to use the first person singular pronoun in a poem?"

Yet it was not a seventeen-year locust just out of the ground who asked, but a woman without exception the most serious-looking I ever saw. She wore pinch-on glasses which seemed to defy anyone or anything to dislodge them, and through the glasses she looked at me with a seriousness that verged on fury.

"Do you consider it permissible to use the first person singular pronoun in a poem?"

Suddenly I felt light-headed. I wanted to mount a table and do a dance. But I restrained myself. The serious woman was asking a perfectly serious question which she had probably asked in other classes, workshops, and clubs where the answer had been sometimes yes and sometimes no. She was merely sounding me out in order to fit me into her framework.

I've regretted ever since that I didn't give her a really thorough answer.

"No, I do not regard it as permissible. And I mean of course not only 'I' but 'my' and 'mine' and 'me.' And 'we,' 'our' and 'us' too. It may surprise you but I do feel it is wiser to omit the second person pronoun as well, both singular and plural."

Then by delicate steps I would have worked up to the point of omitting the third person. Then all pronouns, then nouns. And I could have hinted at still more drastic restrictions.

I see her now as she looked at me through those glasses. Even her gray hair was seriously arranged.

"Do you consider it permissible—?"

✿ Poet as Noble Achievement

In an address at Amherst College in 1959, the distinguished historian, Henry Steele Commager, remarked: "What Amherst student does not know that to be a poet is the noblest achievement of man?"

This brings up the old conundrum: When is a poet a poet and when is a poet not a poet?

When is a poet a poet and when is a poet merely someone who writes poetry? Where lies the dividing line?

If you say that someone who writes poetry but is not a poet doesn't really write poetry at all but rather something else or something less than poetry, something sometimes called "verse," then the question shifts to another. When is poetry poetry and when is poetry not poetry?

But even if we could agree on what poetry is when it really is poetry, would we be willing to agree that everyone who writes it is a poet? A poet, that is, who really is a poet?

Surely Dr. Commager does not mean that each and every writer of poetry or of what passes as poetry is the noblest achievement of man.

If you asked him to name a poet who is the noblest achievement of man, he might name Shakespeare.

That Shakespeare was himself a noble achievement and made a noble achievement no one will deny. But was he any nobler and did he do any more nobly than Michelangelo? Or Johann Sebastian Bach?

Is even the noblest poet any nobler than the noblest philosopher or saint or schoolteacher or historian or carpenter? A *really* noble carpenter? And I mean not just a carpenter who does carpentry however fine, but a carpenter who is a carpenter.

✣ Vacations

Punctually each June the *New Yorker* notifies me that during July and August their poetry department will be closed. "Only topical light verse or poems scheduled for imminent book publication should be submitted during this period."

I wish I knew whether any of their other departments close during the summer and go on vacation. If the poetry department is the only one to shut down, I wish I knew why.

Strange that this should be the first year I have asked these questions or paid much attention to the *New Yorker's* thoughtful annual warning. Perhaps it is because this year I am trying so desperately to get my own poetry department going once again.

❧ The Disillusioning Blurb

A poet has all the poems in his book to prove himself
a poet. But the blurb writer has the last word. On
the back flap of the dust jacket he can reduce the poet
to a brief paragraph of bald prose.

He tells us that the poet was born, and, what is
worse, when and where. To be born is bad enough,
but to be born, say, in Binghamton and in 1906!
Even if such information be not wholly irrelevant, it
imposes severe limitations on the imagination.

If there is any truth in the saying that poets are
born and not made, it is the truth of a second birth.
When a poet is truly born, it is a considerable number
of years after he was born a squalling baby. Of the
baby we can say 1906; but is there any date for the
poet?

Blurb writers seem to have no inkling of this. How
seldom it is that one encounters a blurb writer
worthy of being trusted with the back flap of the
poet's dust jacket. How seldom one ever comes across
anything that approaches the adequate. "The author
of these poems was suckled by a she-wolf, weened on
locusts and wild honey, and is married to seven
goddesses."

❧ A Golden Simplicity?

Have you never noticed how perfectly still some poems lie on the printed page? As the reader's eye brushes over them, as the mind flits across them, they never stir.

This is not to say that they may not be fine poems, well worth an acquaintance. But the reader must wake them up before he can make that acquaintance. The reader must take the initiative.

Perhaps you are glancing through a new anthology not so much to find something to read as just to see what is there. Page after page, poem after poem, until your heart, in spite of you, grows hardened. The more pages you turn the more convinced, yea the more determined, you are that no poem will give you pleasure. Your heart has hardened indeed.

Page after page, poem after poem. Did any of them really want to be written, and not just submit to a poet who wanted to write them? Did all of them really want to be written by a poet?

Page after—then something happens. Something you had forgotten was possible. Your eye is caught by something in the poem before you, some slight movement or the hint of it. And before you know it the poem of its own accord rises from the page and comes toward you!

That day it may well be you turn no more pages.

Later, thinking back, you wonder just what it was about that poem that made it rise from the white page and come toward you. It may be forever impossible to say. A breath of air circulating among the words? A golden simplicity? An arresting candor?

✾ Required Reading

"These are among the truly miraculous works of our time, and ought to be required reading for every beginning poet."

How strangely, how unaccountably, the second part of this sentence follows the first. Miracles, one might suppose, would be sufficiently observed without being required.

But if the reviewer really means what he says, will he kindly tell us what Authority or Establishment, what Academy or Benevolent Despot, would pass such a law?

Furthermore, if this miraculous book is to be made required reading, surely other miraculous books of poetry should be treated likewise—the plays of Shakespeare, for instance, and the *Divine Comedy*. What would be the complete curriculum of required reading for a beginning poet?

By "required reading" I assume the reviewer does not mean actual compulsion. If the beginning poet refused or failed to do his reading, he would be penalized, but no overt force would necessarily be brought to bear.

✿ Professional Poet

Someone the other day called me a professional poet to my face.

"Don't call me that," I cried. "Don't call anybody that. As well talk about a professional friend."

"Oh!" he said.

"Or a professional lover."

"Oh!"

❀ Poetry and Poverty

In his anthology, *The Pleasures of Poverty*, Anthony Bertram makes clear that it is not destitution he is praising. Only a saint can flourish on nothing. But anybody can flourish on enough and no more if he wants to.

The poems and prose selections in his anthology demonstrate that many writers of the past have thought of poverty as something positive. When they praise it, what they are really praising is a very modest, sometimes a ridiculously modest, wealth. Herrick, for instance:

> Here, here I live with what my board
> Can with the smallest cost afford.
> Though n'er so mean the viands be,
> They well content my Prue and me.
> Or pea, or bean, or wort, or beet,
> Whatever comes, content makes sweet.

Today this sort of poverty is not only out of fashion, it is out of mind and perhaps out of existence except in very out-of-the-way places. Today when a man is poor he is poor. He is substandard. And it is not an occasion for congratulation, his own or anybody else's. Robert Herrick's contentment of three centuries ago would be called by another name today.

Yet even so, Herrick may be not altogether irrelevant

to us. A young poet just out of college and not yet married might consider a Herrick sort of life for a few years. With a small income, preferably from part-time work, he could be both comfortable and independent. Like Herrick he could grow the pea, the bean, the wort, the beet, and like Herrick he could keep a hen. Rough clothes, old clothes, would be fine. A good half the day or half the year he could have clear for himself and poetry.

Even if he didn't wholly like such a life, it might be better than going hungry in New York or Paris. He could always move to the city whenever his income permitted. And while living in the country he wouldn't be obliged to write poems in praise of it or in praise of his poverty.

He might, of course, like it. He might decide to stay on. Healthy, solvent, and independent, he might find cottage life good for him, and being good for him good for his poetry as well.

✿ The Indecipherable Poem

I have no love for the indecipherable poem, but for the indecipherable poet I have often a warm friendly feeling. He is usually a bright chap, perhaps brilliant, a good talker, someone worth knowing and worth watching. He is also often a college undergraduate majoring in English and in love with writing.

In his literature and writing courses it is taken for granted that the significant poets are the difficult ones. So, what less can an undergraduate poet do than be difficult himself?

Difficulty, of course, is not the only virtue of great poets. They give us passion, vision, originality. None of these the undergraduate poet probably has, but he *can* be difficult. He can be as difficult as he wants to be. He can be as difficult as anybody else. He need only give the words he uses a private set of meanings. It is not difficult to be difficult.

What I mean is, a poem that is very difficult to read may not have been at all difficult to write.

One poem sufficiently difficult can keep a creative writing class busy a whole hour. If its young author feels pleased with himself, can we blame him? He is human. He has produced something as difficult as anything by Ezra Pound. Why shouldn't he be pleased?

If he wants to, he can let his classmates pick away at his poem indefinitely and never set them straight. If his teacher ventures to criticize a phrase or a line, the author can say that the passage is exactly as he wants it. Is it awkward? Well, he intended it to be awkward since awkwardness was needed at that point. This would be clear, he murmurs, to anyone who understood the poem.

Nobody can touch him. Nobody at all. He is safe. In an ever-threatening world full of old perils and new, such security is to be envied. To be able to sit tight and pretty on top of your poem, impregnable like a little castle perched on a steep rock.

�֎ Electronically Equipped

For some years now I have been intending to have myself electronically equipped for prompt criticism of poems. A card of certain dimensions bearing the poem clearly typed could be deposited in one pocket. Then, after the pushing of a button, another card bearing the criticism would be found in a pocket on the opposite side.

There would be a special button to push for any poet who wanted to make a comment on his poem, such as: "This just came to me. I haven't changed a word."

There would be another button to push for any poet who wanted to ask a specific question, such as: "Should I keep on writing?"

And of course there would be a special pocket from which coins could be recovered if anything had gone amiss with the mechanism.

❀ The Satirical Rogue

I asked the Irish poet if he would be surprised to hear that I was one-quarter Irish myself. Could he tell by looking at me?

After scrutinizing me for a moment, he remarked: "There's something humorous in your right eye."

"My *right* eye?" I cried. "What about my left?"

"That one's more serious," he assured me.

❧ Patience and a Monument

It's a buyer's market, the supply of poetry far exceed-
ing the demand. That is why the buyer can take his
own sweet time in buying or not buying.

He may be a poet himself and know what it is
to be made to wait. Yet in keeping his fellow poets
waiting he is probably not being mean. He is not even
necessarily being inconsiderate. If he is the editor of a
quarterly, it may be convenient for him to let poems
accumulate for a couple of months and then make his
selection from a full net of fishes.

There is something curiously ambivalent about
waiting a long time to hear from an editor. Pessimism
says: If he really liked the poems, surely he would
have given some hint before now. Optimism says:
Why would he hold on to them if he weren't
interested?

Once I was kept waiting considerably more than
one year. The poems had been sent in toward the
end of a certain calendar year, kept all the next year,
and returned early in the third calendar year. I was
reminded of Ephraim Pratt who was born in the
seventeenth century and died in the nineteenth,
having spanned in its entirety the century we are
pleased to call the Enlightenment.

His monument stands on a peaceful slope under
pines in the cemetery of the small town of Shutesbury,
Massachusetts.

Erected by the Town of
Shutesbury in memory of
Ephraim Pratt
Born in East Sudbury
Nov. 1, 1686, Removed to
Shutesbury soon after its
first settlement where
he resided until he
Died May 22, 1804
In his 117 year.
He was remarkably cheer-
ful in his disposition and
temperate in his habits.
He swung a scythe 101 con-
secutive years and mounted a
horse without assistance
at the age of 110.

❧ Poetry and Power

I dreamed that Power and Poetry were walking down the street together. It was beautiful to see how they accommodated themselves to each other. Poetry, for example, walked a little faster than usual and Power slowed down his stride, and so they kept abreast.

I overheard Power tell Poetry that he too was powerful. I could see that Poetry tried not to look flattered and that Power tried not to sound patronizing.

Poetry seemed to hear everything that Power was saying. Communication the other way was not quite so successful, Poetry having a low-pitched voice.

I saw Power reach out a hand as if to lay it on Poetry's shoulder or possibly to pat his head. But the hand couldn't reach head or shoulder. The hand could have reached only if Power had stooped.

They were friends all right, and it was beautiful to see how they kept abreast. They would have gone arm in arm, no doubt, had that been possible.

✤ Logic

If one man's poem is another man's poison, then one man's book of poems is another man's apothecary shop of poisons.

On the other hand, if one man's poison is another man's poem, then one man's apothecary shop of poisons is another man's soda fountain.

✿ John Quincy Adams

We do not think of John Quincy Adams as a poet, yet a volume of his poems was published in 1848, the year of his death. One, "To Sally," is a translation, partly strict and partly freewheeling, of Horace's familiar ode, "Integer Vitae." By doubling the length of each stanza Adams is able to extend Horace's geography magnificently.

> What though he plough the billowy deep
>   By lunar light, or solar,
> Meet the resistless Simoon's sweep
>   Or iceberg circumpolar!
> In bog or quagmire deep and dank
>   His feet shall never settle;
> He mounts the summit of Mount Blanc
>   Or Popocatapetl.

If you remember that early photograph of the old Adams in which he sits staring at us like the incarnation of gloom, or remember the incident told by his grandson Henry of how once the ex-President emerged from his study to grasp the hand of the reluctant boy and lead him every step of the way to school, never once releasing his grip and never once speaking, or remember how in his later years J. Q. rose regularly at five in winter and after starting his chamber fire from flint, began the day with a chapter from his

103

Greek Testament—you are surprised not that he wrote poetry but that he could write it with a light touch. The Horation irony, the mock-seriousness, he catches to a T. Yet I suspect that the seriousness, both with him and with Horace, was not entirely mock. The wolf that ran away may have been all spoofing, but Sally (Lalage) was a lovely girl and no kidding.

"To Sally" may be found in Edmund Clarence Stedman's *An American Anthology*, a monumental work in 878 pages that appeared in 1900. The 590 American nineteenth-century poets included are arranged in eight sections: Early Years of the Nation, First Lyrical Period, Division I, Division II, Division III, Second Lyrical Period, Division I, Division II, Division III, and Close of the Century. John Quincy Adams occurs in Early Years of the Nation, of course. In a very brief biographical note, Stedman calls his verse "quaint and old-fashioned." Could 1848 have seemed as quaint to 1900 as 1900 seems to 1967?

✿ Publisher as Wife

Poets beget poems but publishers give birth to books. Though some men prefer to get along without wives, I never heard of a poet who preferred to get along without a publisher. That many poets do get along without publishers must be attributed to their lack of luck in wooing.

Failing to win a publisher a poet has three choices. (1) He can buy a publisher. (2) He can publish himself. (3) He can remain unpublished.

Buying a publisher may be all right in realms where wives also are for sale. Here in America where wives are at least ostensibly not for sale the buying of a publisher smacks of prostitution.

Being one's own publisher can have the virtue of complete candor. "Published by the author." A poet simply hires a printer. It will do in a pinch, but the pinch should not last too long.

Publishers differ from one another as much as do wives. Some are better housekeepers than others. Some are more affectionate than others. And some do more than others to insure a lasting union. Sometimes a poet and a publisher remain wedded for life. In the lives of other poets there is much divorce—a situation not always necessarily unhappy.

❀ Style

"C——— R——— was the reader for the members' lyric contest poems, looking most stylish in a charming lavender hat and dress."

Let no one look down his nose at this little news item. Surely it was worth noting that the reader looked stylish and that her lavender hat and dress were charming. If her hat and dress were more notable than her style of reading the members' lyric contest poems (to say nothing of the style of the lyric contest poems themselves) it was both honest and sensible to say so.

In her lavender hat and dress what was she but a lyric poem herself?

❧ Poetry as a Competitive Pursuit

It is inevitable, I suppose, that like all other pursuits poetry should be competitive. Inevitable and not altogether unfortunate. Even the angels, it has been intimated, compete with one another for position in the hierarchies and for first prize in holiness.

But is there any virtue in making poetry as competitive as possible? Does poetry flourish necessarily in direct ratio to the number of prizes offered? May not the subtle competition for the esteem of the individual reader be sometimes better than a public competition for lucre?

In a certain Eastern college each April six or seven college students, representing as many colleges, gather to present their own poems to a sympathetic audience. Three judges determine the winner. The winner receives $100, the runner-up $25, and the others nothing. I have often thought how pleasant it would be if no overt judging took place, and if each of the young poets received an honorarium of fifteen or twenty dollars.

❧ The Well-made Poem

Spare me, please, the man who speaks, whether
disparagingly or approvingly, of the well-made poem.
Has he never read or heard that poems are not made
but grow—like snowflakes, like flowers, like seashells?
Has he never perceived that a true poem—like a rose,
like a goddess, like a diamond—is not made but born?

❧ Crowds

Recently the editor of *Epoch*, with the long summer ahead of him, offered his readers a list of the fifty best living American poets. But being a generous man, he did not stop at fifty. His list contained four hundred and thirty-four names.

They were arranged in alphabetical groups. The *S* poets alone numbered fifty-three. There was only one *Z* poet. For *Q* and *Y* there were no poets at all.

The idea seemed to be that from the editor's four hundred and thirty-four the reader could pick his own final fifty.

"I suppose," said a friend of mine, "that a poet might endure being left out of a list of fifty, but to be omitted from a list of four hundred and thirty-four would be unendurable."

"Quite the contrary," I retorted, "if the poet is anything like me. I should feel insulted to be left out of a list of fifty; but if I were omitted from the four hundred and thirty-four, my response would probably be 'Thank God!' "

"Why so?"

"My distaste for crowds."

✿ Modest Check

The Editor sends me his modest check. The phrase is his own. I myself would scarcely have thought of that adjective.

Along with the modest check he writes me a very nice letter. He is clearly a very nice man, check or no check, modest or otherwise. A modest man, I'm sure.

But though modesty is a virtue in human beings, is it necessarily a virtue in checks?

As a check grows larger and larger does it become less and less modest? Does a check too large to be called modest become immodest?

And if there are upper limits to modesty, are there lower limits as well? Just how small may a modest check be and still be modest, rather than measly?

Another question. Why do poets deserve so much modesty?

✤ Group Reviews

They are like mass executions, these group reviews of poetry when there are ten or twelve books in the group. A man can be shot to death with some dignity if he dies alone. To kill ten or twelve in a batch is like swatting flies.

If mass execution be too grim a metaphor, then say a group review is like a group photograph. Good features are lost sight of and weak features thrown into relief. A large head by itself might be impressive but not when surrounded by small heads, or a long nose by short noses.

A book is at a double disadvantage. Good things said about the other books will put it in the shade. Bad things said about the other books easily produce guilt by association.

In a mass review of poetry each poet can be compared to every other poet in the group to the general disadvantage of everybody. Even praise from a group reviewer may be something to fear. "Though X never rises above a certain level of mediocrity, it may be said in his favor that he never falls quite as low as Y."

❋ Yarrow

Having just read three poems by Wordsworth—
"Yarrow Unvisited," "Yarrow Visited," and "Yarrow
Revisited"—I am ready to concede the poet a man
both logical and thorough. The three titles are as
inevitable as beginning, middle, and end; as
comprehensive and comforting as faith, hope, and
charity.

I think I know now what people mean when they
say a writer has exhausted his subject.

Of course, Wordsworth could have written a
fourth poem: "Yarrow Re-revisited." But he didn't.
He knew when to stop.

❧ Weighed in the Balance

"I didn't feel settled quite firmly enough on a choice among these poems," writes the editor of *Poetry*.

An appropriate statement, surely. Honest. Also tactful. I have no complaint.

I am entirely reconciled. Indeed, I am more reconciled than an editor might suppose possible. If there is the least doubt in the editorial mind of the worthiness or suitability of my poem, I much prefer he send it back. I don't want to squeak by. I don't want to creep into the fold.

Perhaps it is pride, but I prefer not to have a poem accepted for any other reason than love. Having known love, now and then, I cannot be content with anything less. Now and again an editor has loved a poem of mine before it was in print, and a reader has loved it afterwards. On such love, on the memory of it, I can live for a while. I can keep going.

Perhaps it is pride, perhaps it is conceit, but I can't keep out of mind the possibility that the poem the editor rejects may have turned the tables on him. While he was judging the poem, the poem may have quietly been judging him. In the eyes of eternity it may be the editor and not the little poem that was weighed in the balance and found wanting.

❊ A Small Door

I would be a translator too, like all the most approved poets, if I could find the right language to translate from. Certainly not French, since everybody already can read the originals. And not Russian, since everybody soon will be able to read the originals. I want a language so remote geographically, linguistically, and spiritually, that not a single poem has ever found its way into English, and might never do so except for my good offices. I want to be a small door connecting two vast but heretofore mutually exclusive worlds.

✤ Other Arts, Other Artists

"Did you ever try to imagine what it would be like
to be a painter?" a poet friend asked me the other day.

"Can't say I ever did," I said.

"Painters fascinate me," he went on. "The way they
work. The way they keep busy. A painter sets up his
easel and sits down and goes to work painting. You
never catch him staring at his canvas, biting his nails."

"Remarkable," I said.

"If a painter is not busy painting, it's because he's
busy doing something else, not because he can't paint.
You see what I'm getting at?"

"Maybe," I said.

"Something keeps guiding him, keeps telling him
what to do next, stroke by stroke. If he's objective,
it's something outside himself. If he's abstract, it's
something inside himself. But something, something
keeps feeding him you might say. And that's not true
of us poets by a long shot—much of the time, at least.
We have to wait, and sometimes we have to wait a
hell of a time."

"For inspiration?" I asked.

"Call it that if you want," he said. "I'd call it simply
a flow of good ideas, and the excitement that comes
from it and that starts other ideas."

"And the burst of confidence," I added.

"What I want to know," he said, "is whether there

has to be this difference, or whether we poets have just got into the habit of thinking there is."

"You mean we pamper ourselves?"

"Not so much pamper as make things hard for ourselves. I wonder if we do. I wonder if we don't."

"You're asking why a poet can't sit down to his typewriter and turn out poems with something like the steadiness with which a painter turns out paintings?"

"Yes, damn it."

"Well, that seems to me just about what some poets are doing."

"I'm not talking about drivel, I'm talking about poetry," he said.

"I'm talking about poetry too. I could name more than one distinguished poet and several not so distinguished who give me the impression they can write a poem almost any time they feel like it. They've learned how to take it easy. They don't try to be brilliant. They just take something nearby or something that happens to come into their mind and set it down with a few little imaginative quirks or touches. I mean they take half a dozen little items and set them down side by side. And somehow it makes a poem. It gives a mood."

"Does that sort of poetry satisfy you?" he asked.

"Not exactly," I said, "but I don't dislike it as much as I do some other kinds."

"Sort of painting with words?"

"I suppose so."

"And here's another thing," he went on. "Painters don't seem to mind being watched at work. They may even like it, find it stimulating. But just imagine you or me working on a poem with somebody hanging over our shoulder. A painter, I tell you, has something to go on so definite that he can keep going even with distractions."

"Painters must have their troubles too," I mused. "For instance, if a painter finds his painting is seriously wrong, there may be nothing to do but scrap it and start all over again. Especially a water color. You or I, now, if we find a poem is not right, we just slip a fresh sheet in the typewriter and write a new version. But take a sculptor now, or a composer. Those are the boys that make me ask questions."

"How so?"

"The way they work on assignment, on commission, turn out work to order. Somebody wants figures for a big fountain, dimensions such and such. Or 'Compose us music for symphony orchestra that will take ten to twelve minutes to play.' Could *you* write a poem to order?"

"God, no! Could you?"

"I don't think I'd want to have to. But maybe we ought to be able and willing and delighted. Maybe we've got into the habit of thinking a poem is not a real poem, not pure, unless it drops out of a clear blue sky. Maybe we're prejudiced."

"Maybe we are," he said. "But I'd say that if we're prejudiced, it's a good prejudice."

"You're going to keep on turning down lucrative commissions?"

"Absolutely."

"And go on staring at a blank sheet of paper in your typewriter and biting your nails?"

"Absolutely."

❧ Peacock

"The successful warrior becomes a chief; the successful
chief becomes a king; his next want is an organ to
disseminate the fame of his achievements and the
extent of his possessions; and this organ he finds in
a bard, who is always ready to celebrate the strength
of his arm, being first duly inspired by that of his
liquor. This is the origin of poetry . . . ."
So wrote Thomas Love Peacock as long ago as 1820.
A satirical rogue, no less.

It was Peacock's essay, "The Four Ages of Poetry,"
that spurred Shelley to his famed "Defense." But
Shelley couldn't touch the rogue, not really.

Too bad Peacock grew shrill and abusive toward the
end of his essay. Bards of the Iron Age he could handle
with a nice irony. But not his contemporaries, no, not
his contemporaries.

Thomas Love Peacock. Or, if you will, plain Tom
Peacock.

❧ In a Brazen World

How often one man is praised in terms of another man's disparagement. You honor Keats by damning Shelley; the more you damn the one the more you honor the other.

But here is something that goes beyond that. Here, on a dust jacket, is a poet praised in terms not of another poet's disparagement, but of all other poets. Only one other poet living, we are informed, can hold a candle to this poet.

> *How far that little candle throws his beams!*
> *So shines a shrill note in a brazen world.*

❁ Slender

"The individual essays in *The Satirical Rogue* are charming indeed, but taken together they make a very slender book, I am afraid," wrote the Senior Editor.

The Senior Editor was commenting on the essays that you are at this moment reading, Dear Reader.

Very well. But why should every book be fat? A slender woman is not usually thought to labor under a disadvantage.

Very well. Very well, indeed. But when were rubies and diamonds sold by the peck?

✿ Introducing the Poet

Theophilus T, my poet-friend, was telling me the other day of various experiences he has had in being introduced to audiences, and of certain strategies he has devised for self-defense.

You see, just at the moment when he wants to be nothing but an inconspicuous vehicle or medium for his poetry, he may find his cap waving with plumes and his pockets bulging with plums.

To remove gracefully as many of the plumes and plums as possible (smiling at himself as he does so and never, of course, at his introducer) has become an art in itself.

Yet having acquired something of a technique, he begins to doubt this whole approach, and for three reasons. (1) No matter how deftly he tries to de-ornament himself and cut himself down to size, he must talk about himself to do so and thus make matters worse. (2) Audiences are so accustomed, he says, to the grand build-up that they take it for granted. He suspects his embarrassment is confined to himself. (3) Audiences may actually like panegyric: the more glory is poured on the head of the poet standing before them, the more reflected glory there will be for everybody to bask in.

Theophilus says he has just about made up his mind that at his next poetry reading he will accept unprotestingly anything and everything the introducer may offer, letting it flow over and off him like rain on the roof or wind through the trees. It will be a peaceful experience, he thinks.